STARK LIBRARY

SEP -- 2022

T4-ADP-481

Dinosaur Graveyards in South America

by Grace Hansen

Abdo Kids Jumbo is an Imprint of Abdo Kids
abdobooks.com

abdobooks.com

Published by Abdo Kids, a division of ABDO, P.O. Box 398166, Minneapolis, Minnesota 55439. Copyright © 2022 by Abdo Consulting Group, Inc. International copyrights reserved in all countries. No part of this book may be reproduced in any form without written permission from the publisher. Abdo Kids Jumbo™ is a trademark and logo of Abdo Kids.

Printed in the United States of America, North Mankato, Minnesota.

102021

012022

THIS BOOK CONTAINS RECYCLED MATERIALS

Photo Credits: Alamy, Getty Images, iStock, Science Source, Shutterstock, ©Marcio L. Castro p9 / CC BY-SA 4.0, ©Kabacchi p11 / CC BY 2.0, ©Marcos A. F. Sales, Cesar L. Schultz p15 / CC BY 4.0

Production Contributors: Teddy Borth, Jennie Forsberg, Grace Hansen
Design Contributors: Candice Keimig, Pakou Moua

Library of Congress Control Number: 2021940140
Publisher's Cataloging-in-Publication Data

Names: Hansen, Grace, author.
Title: Dinosaur graveyards in South America / by Grace Hansen
Description: Minneapolis, Minnesota : Abdo Kids, 2022 | Series: Dinosaur graveyards | Includes online resources and index.
Identifiers: ISBN 9781098209490 (lib. bdg.) | ISBN 9781098260200 (ebook) | ISBN 9781098260552 (Read-to-Me ebook)
Subjects: LCSH: Dinosaurs--Juvenile literature. | Fossils--Juvenile literature. | South America--Juvenile literature. | Paleontology--Juvenile literature. | Paleontological excavations--Juvenile literature.
Classification: DDC 567--dc23

Table of Contents

Dinosaurs of South America 4

Caturrita Formation. 8

Santa Maria Formation 10

Romualdo Formation 14

Huincul Formation. 16

Lecho Formation 18

Candeleros Formation 20

Some Major Dinosaur Groups . . 22

Glossary 23

Index 24

Abdo Kids Code. 24

Dinosaurs of South America

Dinosaurs lived between 245 and 66 million years ago. After a dinosaur's death, its remains could turn to fossil if the conditions were perfect. This process takes more than 10,000 years!

5

Every continent has dinosaur fossils, including South America. Fossils are often found in **rock formations**. Some formations hold more remains than others!

Caturrita Formation

Brazil's Caturrita Formation holds the fossils of Sacisaurus. It had strong legs. It could probably run fast!

Sacisaurus

- Ornithopod
- Late Triassic
- Herbivore
- About the size of a park bench

Brazil
Caturrita Formation
South America

Santa Maria Formation

Fossils belonging to one of the earliest dinosaurs was found in the Santa Maria Formation. It was a small and fast **predator**.

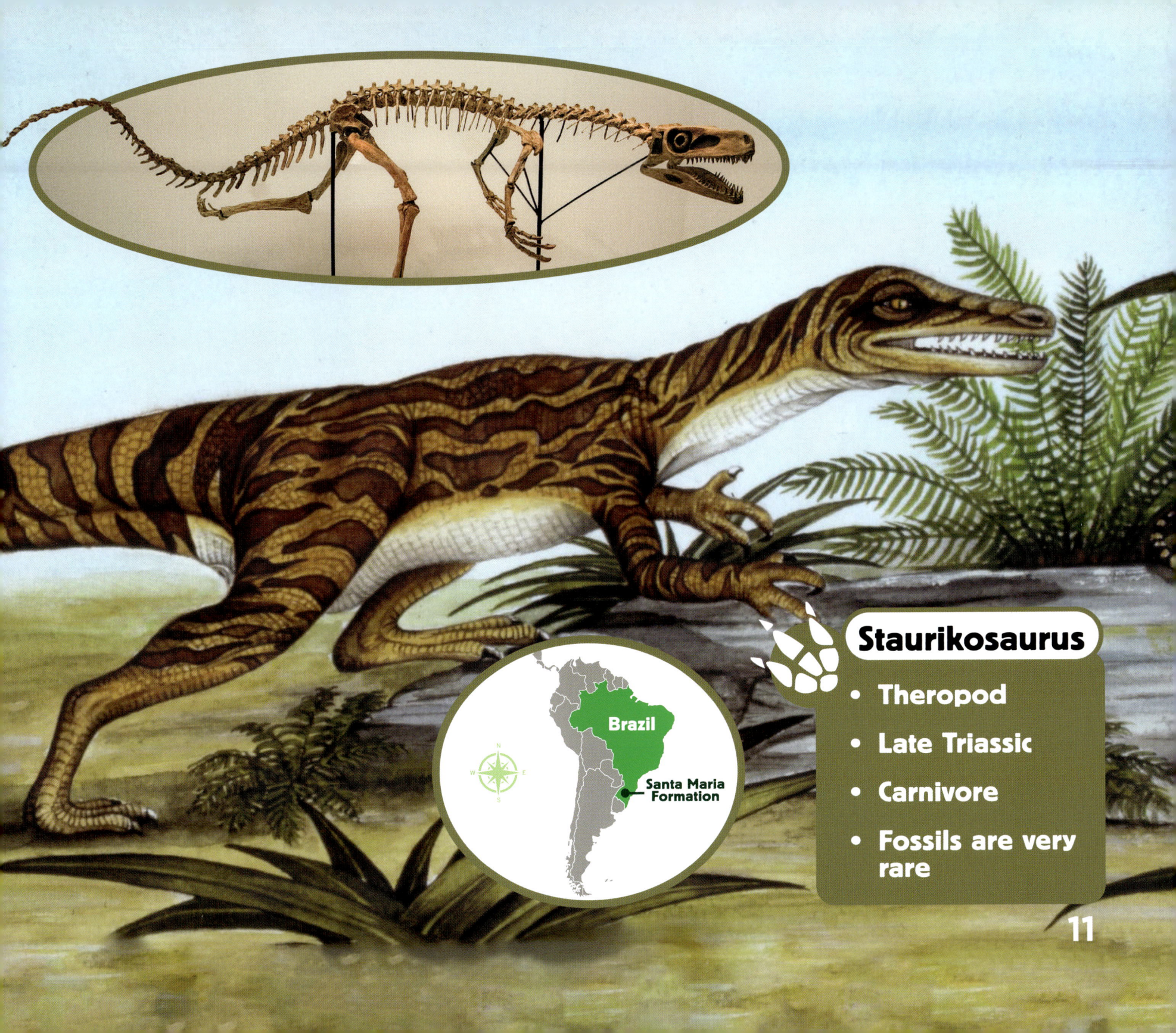

Staurikosaurus

- Theropod
- Late Triassic
- Carnivore
- Fossils are very rare

Ancient reptile fossils have been uncovered there too. This animal had a beak and a strong, bulky body.

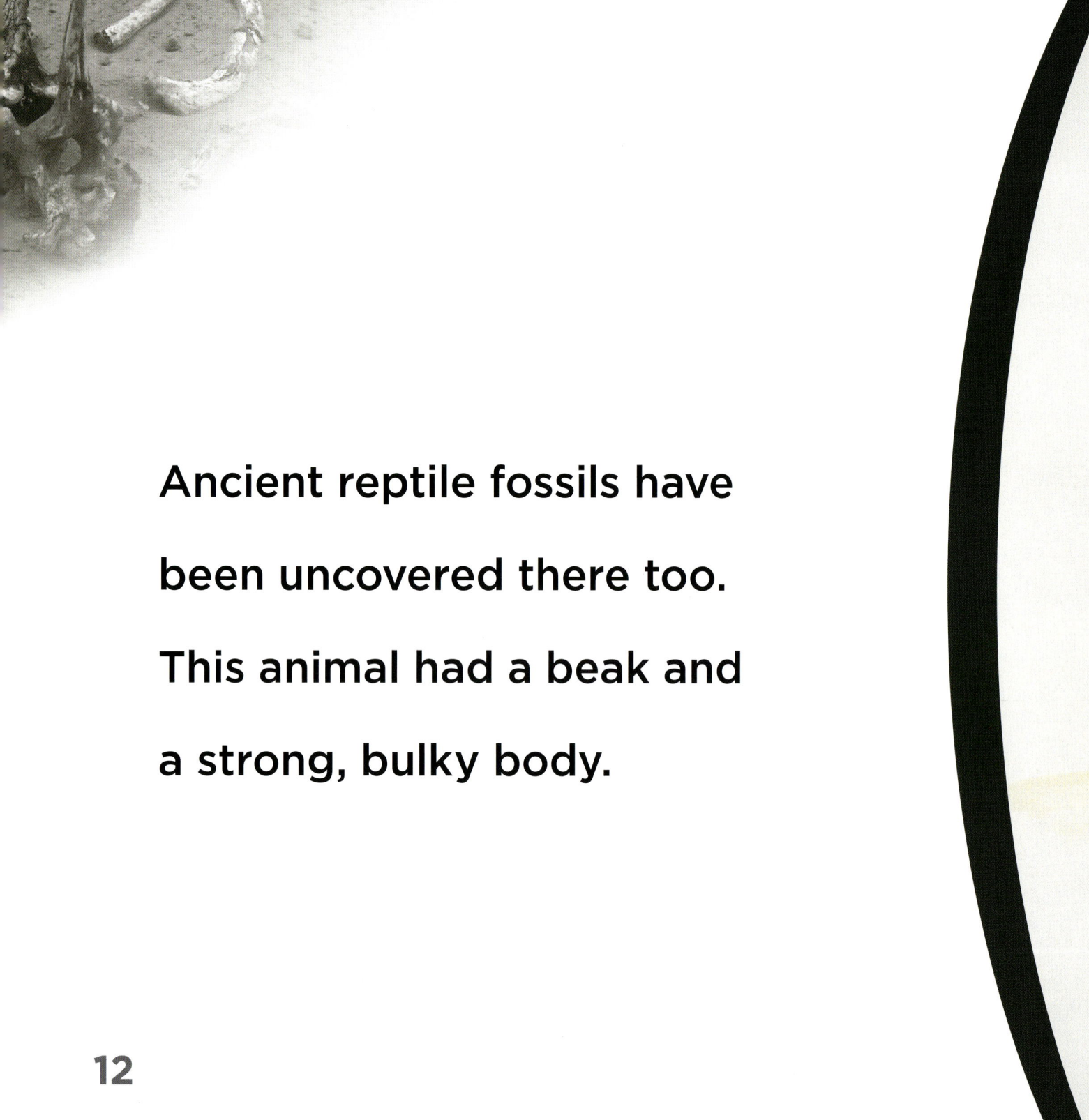

Hyperodapedon
- Rhynchosaur
- Late Triassic
- Herbivore
- Large teeth likely helped break open seeds

Romualdo Formation

The Romualdo Formation is well known. There, a nearly complete Irritator skull was discovered.

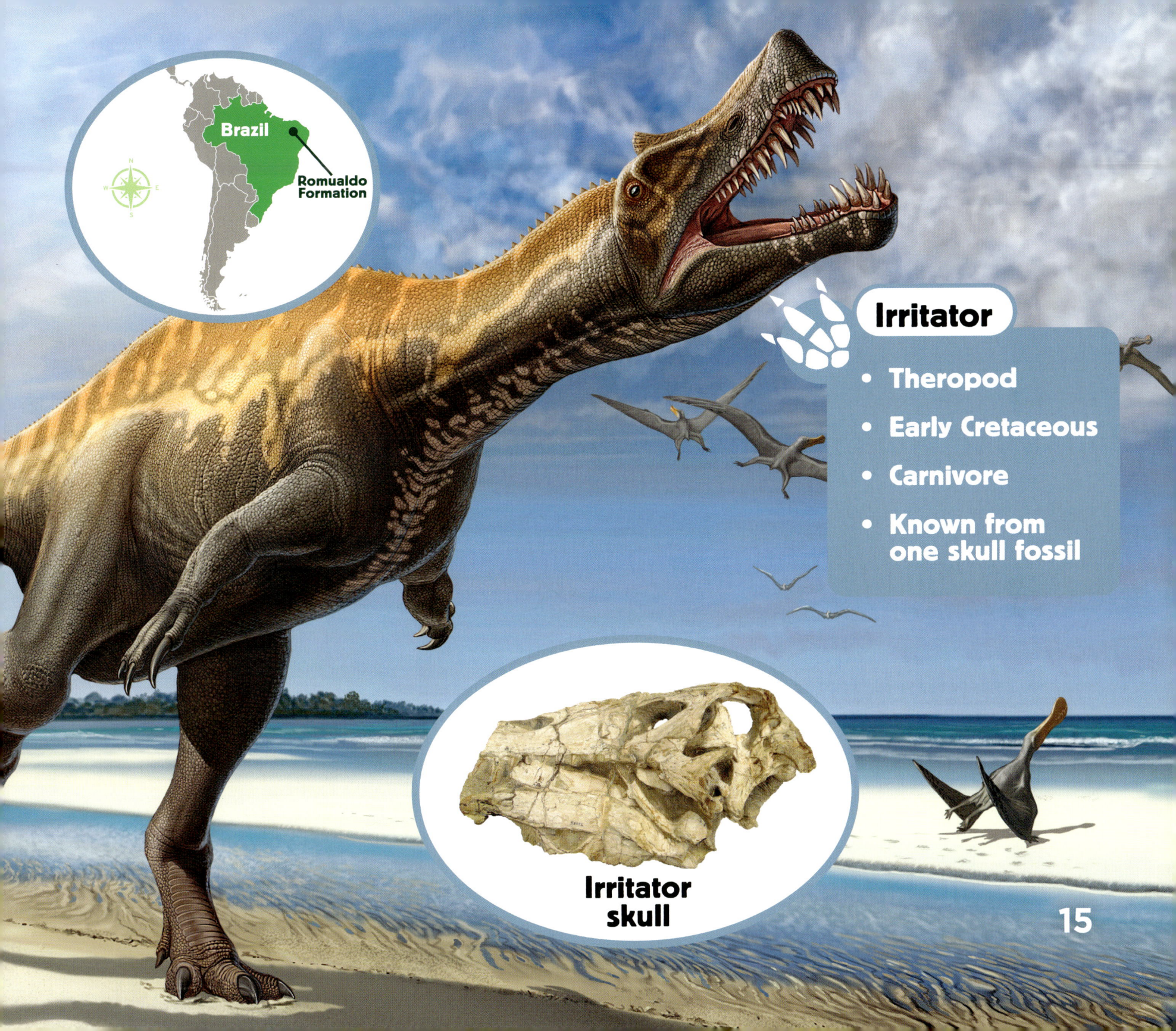

Irritator

- Theropod
- Early Cretaceous
- Carnivore
- Known from one skull fossil

Irritator skull

15

Huincul Formation

Argentina is filled with dinosaur fossils. The Huincul Formation held one of the largest land animals to ever live.

Argentinosaurus

- Sauropod
- Late Cretaceous
- Herbivore
- Nearly half the length of a football field

Lecho Formation

Saltasaurus was small compared to other sauropods. Some of its remains were found in the Lecho Formation. A small theropod was dug up there too.

Noasaurus
- Theropod
- Late Cretaceous
- Carnivore
- Length of a twin mattress

Saltasaurus
- Sauropod
- Late Cretaceous
- Herbivore
- Covered with bony plates

Lecho Formation

Argentina

Candeleros Formation

The Candeleros Formation held an amazing discovery. It was a **carnivore** even larger than Tyrannosaurus rex!

Giganotosaurus

- Theropod
- Late Cretaceous
- Carnivore
- About the length of a telephone pole
- First unearthed in 1993

Giganotosaurus jaw with teeth

21

Some Major Dinosaur Groups

Ankylosauria
- Four-legged
- Heavily armored
- Tank-like
- Some members had clubbed tails
- Herbivores

Ceratopsia
- Four-legged
- Solidly built
- Enormous skulls
- Long horns
- Sharp beaks
- Herbivores

Ornithischia

Ornithopoda
- Two-legged
- Beaked
- Had cheek teeth
- Herbivores

Stegosauria
- Four-legged
- Small heads
- Heavy, bony plates with sharp spikes down the backbone
- Herbivores

Sauropoda
- Four-legged
- Very large
- Long necks and tails
- Small heads
- Herbivores

Saurichia

Theropoda
- Two-legged
- From small and delicate to very large in size
- Small arms
- Carnivores and omnivores

Glossary

carnivore – an animal that eats the flesh of other animals.

herbivore – an animal that feeds only on plants.

omnivore – an animal that eats both plants and other animals.

predator – an animal that hunts other animals for food.

rock formation – a large body of rock that has a consistent set of physical characteristics that make it standout from other bodies of rock nearby.

Index

Argentina 16, 18, 20

Argentinosaurus 16, 17

Brazil 8, 10, 12, 14

Giganotosaurus 20, 21

Hyperodapedon 12, 13

Irritator 14, 15

Noasaurus 18, 19

Sacisaurus 8, 9

Saltasaurus 18, 19

Staurikosaurus 10, 11

Tyrannosaurus rex 20

Visit **abdokids.com** to access crafts, games, videos, and more!

Use Abdo Kids code **DDK9490** or scan this QR code!

24

3 1333 05175 1905